MY FIRST

MALAWI

ALL ABOUT MALAWI FOR KIDS

GLOBED
CHILDREN BOOKS

Interior and cover Design: Daniel Day
Editor: Margaret Bam

For My Sons, Daniel, David and Jude

Shore of Lake Malawi, Malawi

Malawi

Malawi is a **country**.

A country is land that is controlled by a **single government**. Countries are also called **nations, states, or nation-states**.

Countries can be **different sizes**. Some countries are big and others are small.

Female farmer in Malawi

Where Is Malawi?

Malawi is located in the continent of Africa.

A continent is a massive area of land that is separated from others by water or other natural features.

Malawi is situated in South-eastern Africa.

City Mall in Lilongwe

Capital

The capital of Malawi is Lilongwe.

Lilongwe is located in the **central part** of the country.

Lilongwe is the largest city in Malawi.

Elephant Rock, Malawi

Districts

Malawi is divided into 28 districts

The districts of Malawi are as follows

Chitipa, Karonga, Likoma, Mzimba, Nkhata Bay, Rumphi, Dedza, Dowa, Kasungu, Lilongwe, Mchinji, Nkhotakota, Ntcheu, Ntchisi, Salima, Balaka, Blantyre, Chikwawa, Chiradzulu, Machinga, Mangochi, Mulanje, Mwanza, Nsanje, Thyolo, Phalombe, Zomba and Neno.

Population

Malawi has a population of around **20 million people** making it the 21st most populated country in Africa and the 62nd most populated country in the world.

Baobab tree in Malawian village

Size

Malawi is **118,484 square kilometres** making it the 99th largest country in the world by area. Malawi is the 36th largest country in Africa.

Languages

The official language of Malawi is English. Chewa is a popular language in Malawi and is spoken by roughly 40 per cent of the population.

There are many other languages spoken in Malawi such as Tumbuka, Lomwe, Yao, Ngoni, Sena, Mang'anja and Nyanja.

Here are a few phrases and sayings in Chewa
- **Takulandirani** - Welcome
- **Ndili bwino** - I'm fine

Liwonde National Park

Attractions

There are lots of interesting places to see in Malawi.

Some beautiful places to visit in Malawi are

- **Majete Wildlife Reserve**
- **Liwonde National Park**
- **Lilongwe Wildlife Centre**
- **Chongoni Rock Art Area**
- **Lake Malawi National Park**
- **Mulanje Massif**

Likoma Island, Lake Malawi

History of Malawi

People have lived in Malawi for a very long time. In fact, the area now known as Malawi had a small population of hunter-gatherers before waves of Bantu peoples in the 10th century.

In the late 17th century, the territory was colonised by the British and became a protectorate of the United Kingdom known as Nyasaland.

Malawi gained independence from the United Kingdom on 6th July 1966.

Village in Malawi

Customs in Malawi

Malawi has many fascinating customs and traditions.

- Music and dance plays a very important role in Malawian culture. While the various tribes have their own dance forms; the Gule Wamakulu is the most famous of the traditional Malawian dances.
- Family is an important part of Malawian culture. Malawian families have a great sense of community, sharing all duties and chores. Families live in close proximity looking after one another.

Music of Malawi

There are many different music genres in Malawi such as Kwela Music, Malawian jazz, Malawian kwasa kwasa and Malawian hip-hop/rap.

Some notable Malawian musicians include
- Gwamba
- George Kalukusha
- Tay Grin
- Giddess Chalamanda
- Wambali Mkandawire

Food of Malawi

Malawian food is known for being tasty, delicious and flavoursome.

The national dish of Malawi is **Malawian Nshima** which is made from pounded white maize

Woman washing rice in Malawi

Food of Malawi

Some popular dishes in Malawi include

- **Mgaiwa Phala**
- **Kondowole**
- **Nsima**
- **Shum/Sumu**
- **Kholowa**
- **Grilled fish**
- **Mkhwani**
- **Zitumbuwa**

African farmer in Malawi

Weather in Malawi

Malawi has a **sub-tropical climate** characterized by two seasons: the cool dry season between May and October and the hot wet season between November and April.

Herd of African Elephants in Malawi

Animals of Malawi

There are many wonderful animals in Malawi.

Here are some animals that live in Malawi

- African Elephant
- Yellow Baboon
- Hippopotamus
- Spotted Hyena
- Greater Kudu
- Lesser Flamingo

Long waterfall in the Jungle near Livingstonia in Malawi

Waterfalls

There are many beautiful waterfalls in Malawi which is one of the reasons why so many people visit this beautiful country every year.

Here are some of Malawi's waterfall

- Manchewe Waterfalls
- Kapichira Falls
- Likhubula Falls
- Machinjiri Waterfalls

Malawi football

Sports in Malawi

Sports play an integral part in Malawian culture. The most popular sport is Football.

Here are some of famous sportspeople from Malawi

- Gabadinho Mhango - Football
- Tabitha Chawinga - Football
- Taonere Banda - Athletics
- Robert Ng'ambi - Football
- Peter Mponda - Football

Lake Malawi

Famous

Many successful people hail from Malawi.

Here are some notable Malawian figures

- **Frank Chipasula – Writer**
- **Joyce Banda – President**
- **James Sangala – Footballer**
- **William Kamkwamba – Writer**

Lilongwe, Malawi

Something Extra...

As a little something extra, we are going to share some lesser known facts about Malawi

- The tobacco of Malawi is found in almost all cigarette blends including well-known brands like Marlboro.
- Lake Malawi was once called "The Lake of Stars".

Malawian woman

Words From the Author

We hope that you enjoyed learning about the wonderful country of Malawi.

Malawi is a country rich in culture and beauty, with lots of wonderful places to visit and people to meet.

We hope you continue to learn more about this wonderful nation. If you enjoyed this book, consider leaving a review!

With Love

Printed in Great Britain
by Amazon